**HEINEMANN STATE STUDIES**

# Uniquely New Hampshire

Peter Melman

**Heinemann Library**
Chicago, Illinois

Designed by Heinemann Library
Printed in China by WKT Company Limited.

08 07 06 05 04
10 9 8 7 6 5 4 3 2 1

**Library of Congress
Cataloging-in-Publication Data**

Melman, Peter.
  Uniquely New Hampshire / Peter Melman.
    p. cm. — (Heinemann state studies)
Includes index.
  ISBN 1-4034-4651-2 (hc library binding)—
ISBN 1-4034-4720-9 (pb)
  1.  New Hampshire—Juvenile literature.
I. Title. II. Series.
  F34.3.M45 2004
  974.2—dc22

                            2004002773

**Acknowledgments**

Development and photo research by
BOOK BUILDERS LLC

The author and publishers are grateful to the
following for permission to reproduce copyright
material:

Cover photographs by (top, L-R): Joseph Mehling/
Dartmouth; Dave G. Houser/Corbis; Joe Sohm/
Alamy; Lee Snider/Corbis; (main): Laura C.
Scheibel; Title page (L-R): Tim McMahon, Laura C.
Scheibel; Contents: Courtesy New Hampshire
Tourism; p. 4, 7, 10, 26, 29, 31, 39, 40, 41, 43, 44
Laura C. Scheibel; p. 5 John Mitterholzer; p. 6, 30,
38 Tim McMahon; p. 8, 42, 45 Maps by IMA for
BOOK BUILDERS LLC; p. 9 Dave G. Houser/Corbis;
p. 11T Joe Sohm/Alamy; p. 11B, 13T, 13B, 14T,
16T, Courtesy New Hampshire Tourism; p. 13M,
16B, 17T, 18 Alamy; p. 14M, 14B Courtesy New
Hampshire Fish & Game; p. 15T, 15B USFWS; p.
16M Ann B. Swengel/USFWS; p. 17M, 19, 22, 23,
24, 28 New Hampshire Historical Society; p. 21 Lee
Snider/Corbis; p. 32 Barbara Minton for Heinemann Library; p. 33 R. Capozzelli for Heinemann
Library; p. 35 Courtesy Media Relations University
of New Hampshire; p. 36 Solstice Photography/
Alamy; p. 37 Pictor
International/Alamy.

Special thanks to Bill Kellogg of the World Affairs
Council of New Hampshire and the New Hampshire Historical Society for his expert comments in
the preparation of this book.

Every effort has been made to contact copyright
holders of any material reproduced in this book.
Any omissions will be rectified in subsequent
printings if notice is given to the publisher.

**Cover Pictures**

**Top** (left to right) Dartmouth; Mount Washington cog railway; New Hampshire state
flag; statue of Daniel Webster **Main** Mount
Washington Hotel

Some words are shown in bold, **like this.**
You can find out what they mean by looking
in the glossary.

# Contents

# Uniquely New Hampshire

**N**ew Hampshire is unique, a one-of-a-kind state. It was the first of the thirteen colonies to declare its independence from Great Britain. It is also the birthplace of the first U.S. astronaut, Alan B. Shepard, Jr. and of the world's first alarm clock. These are just a few of the facts that make New Hampshire unique.

*In 1806, Governor John Langdon convinced the New Hampshire legislature to settle in Concord. Before that time, the legislature met in eight different towns. Once a permanent home was selected, work began on the state house, which was built of granite on land donated by the people of Concord.*

## ORIGIN OF THE STATE'S NAME

Captain John Mason, a businessperson who founded the Company of Laconia, named New Hampshire in 1622. He named it after his birthplace, Hampshire County, England. Thanks to the company's clever planning, the colony of New Hampshire soon became successful.

## MAJOR CITIES

Today, New Hampshire contains several large cities, three of which are located in the Merrimack River valley.

One of these cities is Concord, the state capital, home to more than 40,000 people. Lawmakers

chose Concord as the capital in 1808. The New Hampshire senate chamber in the state capitol building is the nation's oldest legislative chamber still being used. Its doors first opened in 1819.

Also located on the Merrimack River, Manchester is New Hampshire's largest city, with about 107,000 people. It was home to the Amoskeag Manufacturing Company, which was the largest **textile** mill in the world in the mid-1800s and the early 1900s. Today, Manchester, which continues to be the center for modern industry in the state, produces computers, electrical machines, plastics, and manufactured metal.

Farther south on the Merrimack River is Nashua, situated on the Massachusetts border. Because of its location, many of its 86,000 residents commute to work in Boston, Massachusetts, 40 miles away. Nashua is a popular shopping destination for people who drive up from Massachusetts to avoid that state's sales tax. Like Manchester, Nashua was once a mill town but has since grown into a center for high technology. Voted *Money Magazine*'s "Best Place to Live in America" in 1987 and 1997, Nashua celebrated its 150th anniversary in 2003.

· · · · · · · · · · · · · · · · · · · · · · · · ·

*Nashua, the second largest city in New Hampshire, was a bustling manufacturing city in the 1800s. This former mill is today a restaurant specializing in Mexican food.*

# New Hampshire's Geography and Climate

**N**ew Hampshire is shaped like a northward-pointing piece of pie with a small bite taken from the tip. The state, located in the northeastern United States, is the seventh smallest in the country. The top of the state borders the Canadian province of Quebec. Maine and the Atlantic Ocean share New Hampshire's eastern border. On its western border is Vermont. To the south, the state borders Massachusetts.

*At this lake in the White Moutains, the fall leaves change from green to bright orange, yellow, gold, and red.*

## LAND

New Hampshire has four main regions. The Coastal Lowlands are in the southeastern part of the state, the Monadnock Region is in the southwest corner, the Eastern New England Uplands are west of the Coastal Lowlands, and the White Mountains region is the farthest north.

In New Hampshire, the Coastal Lowlands begin on the Atlantic coast and reach inland between fifteen and twenty miles. The

lowlands possess many rivers and good farmland. It was the first region of New Hampshire to be settled, thanks to the rich soil and fishing off the coast. An important city located in the Coastal Lowlands is Portsmouth, long known for its shipbuilding industry.

*On April 12, 1934, at the summit of Mount Washington, wind speeds reached 231 mph, the highest speeds recorded on Earth.*

The Monadnock Region has small towns with village squares, farmlands, and lush greenery. The villages let visitors see how New England was years ago. The region has many antique stores and small museums, plus six covered bridges.

The Eastern New England Uplands stretch from Maine to eastern Connecticut. In New Hampshire, the uplands are broken into three main areas: the Merrimack valley, the Hills and Lakes area, and the Connecticut River valley. One noteworthy feature in the uplands is Lake Winnipesaukee, located in the Lakes area. The largest lake in the state, it covers 72 square miles and contains 274 islands.

The White Mountains region of New Hampshire, in the northern part of the state, is home to many rugged peaks and valleys, including Mount Washington, the tallest mountain in the state at 6,288 feet. Every year skiers come to Mount Washington to ski its snow-packed slopes.

## A CONTINENTAL CLIMATE

New Hampshire has four distinct seasons. The climate is greatly influenced by the Atlantic Ocean, as well as by the mountains and lakes within the state. In summer, New Hampshire is generally warm and sunny during the day, with temperatures averaging in the seventies

## Average Annual Precipitation
## New Hampshire

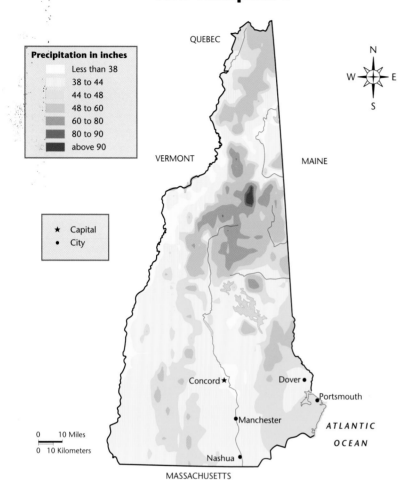

**Precipitation in inches**
- Less than 38
- 38 to 44
- 44 to 48
- 48 to 60
- 60 to 80
- 80 to 90
- above 90

★ Capital
• City

QUEBEC
VERMONT
MAINE
Concord ★
Dover •
Portsmouth
• Manchester
ATLANTIC
OCEAN
Nashua •
MASSACHUSETTS

0    10 Miles
0    10 Kilometers

N
W — E
S

Fahrenheit, while the nights average between 50°F and 60°F. In the fall, the leaves in New Hampshire change from green to bright orange, yellow, gold, and red. Leaf colors are bolder in New Hampshire and other New England states because of the climate, location, and types of trees found there. The temperatures in fall are crisp, dropping in daily average from 60°F in September to 25°F in December. Winters in New Hampshire are cold, with long periods when temperatures remain below freezing, often with great amounts of snow. The daily temperatures in April and May are still chilly, averaging between 44°F and 56°F.

## PRECIPITATION—RAIN AND SNOW

New Hampshire's rainfall averages about 3.2 inches per month, totaling about 42 inches a year. During a typical New Hampshire winter, snow will be on the ground until late March. The southern part of the state averages between 50 to 70 inches of snow each winter, while the northern part averages between 60 and 100 inches. In fact, it is possible for a mountain hike in August to be interrupted suddenly by a snowstorm, although the snow quickly melts.

# Famous Firsts

**N**ew Hampshire is home to many firsts. In 1719 the first potato was planted in the United States at Londonderry Common Field in Derry. Potatoes soon provided every colony with a steady supply of food.

On January 5, 1776, at the Fifth Provincial Congress—a meeting of colonial **delegates**—New Hampshire became the first state to declare itself free from British rule. Until this time, the colonies were subject to the laws that England passed for them.

Also at the Fifth Provincial Congress, New Hampshire became the first of the colonies to adopt a state constitution, a document that set up the rules for **self-government.** The delegates chose not to follow the laws of the British **monarchy** any longer. Instead they decided that the people of New Hampshire should rule themselves.

In 1833, Peterborough established the first free public library in the United States. Sixteen years later, New Hampshire passed the first general library law, which allowed local governments to raise taxes to support libraries. This law also required libraries to be open to all citizens, no matter what their color, religion, or **ethnic** background.

In 1869, New Hampshire became home to the first mountain-climbing cog railroad, which was built up the side of the state's highest

*To build the cog railway, equipment and materials were hauled for 31 miles by teams of oxen.*

*The five-minute Aerial Tramway ride is one way to begin a hike to Cannon Mountain's summit at 4,060 feet.*

• • • • • • • • • • • • • • • • • • • • • • •

peak, Mount Washington. A cog railroad is different from a regular railroad. A cog railroad has a cogwheel, which is attached under the body of the locomotive and grips a center rail.

In 1938, Franconia Notch at Cannon Mountain became the site of the first aerial passenger tramway in North America. This device, a passenger car attached to an overhead cable, allows people to travel over difficult terrain, such as a steep valley, without needing a bridge.

In 1947, New Hampshire firefighters near Concord were the first in the world to use artificial rain to fight forest fires. This idea helped save many lives and millions of dollars of property. Since then, it has become widely adopted throughout the world.

In 1952, New Hampshire held the first presidential primary election. A primary election is one in which candidates of the same political party compete to be their party's candidate for office. Today, the New Hampshire presidential primary is the earliest one held in the year of a presidential election. Candidates come to New Hampshire to become better known and to gain popular support.

# New Hampshire's State Symbols

## NEW HAMPSHIRE STATE FLAG

The New Hampshire state flag was designed in 1784, officially adopted in 1909, and revised in 1931. It displays the New Hampshire state seal on a dark blue background.

*Surrounding the state seal is a yellow laurel wreath and nine yellow stars, signifying that New Hampshire became the ninth state of the Union in 1788.*

## NEW HAMPSHIRE STATE SEAL

The New Hampshire state seal, designed in 1784, depicts the ship *Raleigh,* a granite boulder, a rising sun, and a laurel wreath. The laurel wreath surrounding the ship signifies victory. New Hampshire adopted its first constitution in 1776.

*The* Raleigh *was built in only 60 days in 1776 to fight against the British. It symbolizes the willingness of New Hampshirites to struggle for their beliefs.*

## STATE MOTTO: LIVE FREE OR DIE

In 1809, the **Revolutionary War** hero John Stark coined the phrase Live Free or Die. It became New Hampshire's official state motto in 1945. The motto appears on the state's license plates.

## STATE NICKNAME: THE GRANITE STATE

New Hampshire's nickname is the Granite State. Early settlers to New Hampshire found large deposits of granite there. Granite, a rock used in building construction, is still New Hampshire's most famed natural resource.

## State Song: "Old New Hampshire"

With a skill that knows no measure,
From the golden store of Fate
God, in His great love and wisdom,
Made the rugged Granite State;
Made the lakes, the fields, the forests;
Made the Rivers and the rills;
Made the bubbling, crystal fountains
Of New Hampshire's Granite Hills.

Old New Hampshire, Old New Hampshire
Old New Hampshire Grand and Great
We will sing of Old New Hampshire,
Of the dear old Granite State.

## STATE SONG: "OLD NEW HAMPSHIRE"

The New Hampshire state song, "Old New Hampshire," was written by Dr. John F. Holmes in 1926. The state legislature adopted it as the official state song in 1949.

## STATE FLOWER: PURPLE LILAC

The purple lilac was first planted at the Portsmouth home of Governor Benning Wentworth in 1750. A very **hardy** plant, it symbolizes the rugged personality of the people of New Hampshire. The purple lilac became the state flower in 1919.

*Several flowers other than the purple lilac were considered for the state flower, including the apple blossom and the buttercup. Finally, the purple lilac was chosen as a symbol of the "hardy character of the men and women of the Granite State."*

## STATE WILDFLOWER: PINK LADY SLIPPER

The pink lady slipper is native to New Hampshire and thrives in the state's wooded areas. It became the state wildflower in 1991.

## STATE TREE: WHITE BIRCH

The white birch is native to New Hampshire and grows in every region of the state. It is also known as the canoe birch or paper birch because Native Americans once used it to build canoes. White birches are graceful trees that grow up to 80 feet tall. The white birch became the official state tree in 1947.

*The pink lady slipper blooms from spring to fall.*

## STATE BIRD: PURPLE FINCH

The purple finch is actually a reddish color and is about six inches long. A common bird found throughout much of the United States, it lives in woodland

*Many of New Hampshire's forests, such as the White Mountain National Forest, are home to the tall and strong white birch.*

*Male purple finches have purplish-red heads. Females have brown crowns.*

areas as well as in the suburbs. It became the state bird in 1957.

## STATE MAMMAL: WHITE-TAILED DEER

The white-tailed deer is the most plentiful and widely distributed big-game animal in North America. Often hunted, it lives in wooded areas, including those of New Hampshire. Students at Gossler Park School in Manchester nominated the white-tailed deer to be the state mammal. The state legislature made it official in 1983.

## STATE AMPHIBIAN: SPOTTED NEWT

The spotted newt lives in grassy or weedy ponds and eats insects. New Hampshire residents appreciate these **amphibians** because they eat mosquito eggs. Adults are

*Only male white-tailed deer have antlers. They lose them in the late winter and grow new ones during the spring.*

*Related to the salamander, the spotted newt inhabits New Hampshire's streams and rivers, as well as many collectors' aquariums.*

olive green with a yellow belly and small red spots along their back. Students from Goffstown High in Goffstown, New Hampshire, proposed the spotted newt as the state amphibian. In 1985, the legislature made it official.

## STATE FRESHWATER FISH: BROOK TROUT

The brook trout, which became the state freshwater fish in 1994, lives in New Hampshire's cold, pure streams and lakes. It is a popular sport fish, averaging ten to twelve inches in length and weighing one to four pounds.

## STATE SALTWATER FISH: STRIPED BASS

The striped bass became the state saltwater fish in 1994. It is known for its fighting ability and size—it can weigh up to 100 pounds and reach 5 feet long. It is one of the most prized saltwater fish not only because of its size and strength but also because of its taste.

## STATE INSECT: LADYBUG

The ladybug is a small round beetle, which is usually bright red or yellow and speckled with black, white, or yellow spots. Because ladybugs feast on insects that damage fruit crops, such as New Hampshire apples, fruit-growing farmers greatly appreciate them. The ladybug became the state insect

*Brook trout will not survive if the water temperature rises above 68°F in the summer.*

*The striped bass lives in the Atlantic Ocean, in an area ranging from northern Florida to the Saint Lawrence River in southern Canada.*

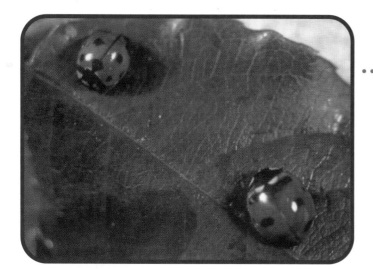

in 1977 when students from Broken Ground School suggested it.

## STATE BUTTERFLY: KARNER BLUE BUTTERFLY

The Karner blue butterfly, also known as the Melissa blue, became the state butterfly in 1992. It is a small butterfly, with a one-inch wingspan. The male has violet-blue wings fringed with white, while the female's wings are brownish blue with orange spots. It relies on the wild lupine flower for food.

## STATE MINERAL: BERYL

Beryl, or beryllium aluminum silicate, is found in granite rocks and is plentiful in New Hampshire. It became the state mineral in 1985.

*The Karner blue butterfly is in danger of extinction because its major food source is disappearing.*

*Beryl is found in many colors—green, blue-green, yellow, pink, and red.*

## State Gem: Smoky Quartz

Like beryl, smoky **quartz** is commonly found in granite, the state rock of New Hampshire. Because so few other gemstones are brown or black, smokey quartz is easy to identify. It became the state gem in 1985.

Smoky quartz is often used as a decorative stone.

## State Rock: Granite

Granite, a light gray rock mined in **quarries,** is made up mostly of quartz and **feldspar.** Because it can withstand great pressure (15,000 to 20,000 pounds per square inch), it is very strong. Granite is often used in the construction of buildings and bridges. It is also used for monuments because it does not damage easily and remains smooth when polished. Granite became the state rock in 1985.

New Hampshire granite was used in the Washington Monument in Washington, D.C., and in the Brooklyn Bridge in New York City.

## New Hampshire State Quarter

Minted in 2000, the New Hampshire state quarter is the ninth coin in the state quarter series. The main image on the back of the coin is the Old Man of the Mountain, a famous rock formation in the White Mountains. Unfortunately, this symbol of the state collapsed in 2003.

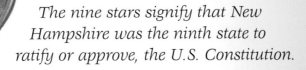

The nine stars signify that New Hampshire was the ninth state to ratify or approve, the U.S. Constitution.

# New Hampshire's History & People

*King James became the king of Scotland in 1567. He became the king of England in 1603 and reigned until 1625.*

**T**he story of New Hampshire goes back to prehistory—a time before anything was written down. For centuries, groups of Native Americans traveled the rivers and lakeshores of the area that is now New Hampshire. They fished, hunted, and planted crops. Because these early people had no written language, **archaeologists** have learned about them by studying their settlements and **artifacts.**

## EARLY EXPLORERS

In 1603, a 23-year-old Englishman, Martin Pring, became the first known European to lead an expedition to what would become New Hampshire. Later, in 1622, King James I of England granted Captain John Mason's request to found and develop, along with Sir Ferdinando Gorges, the Company of Laconia in present-day New Hampshire. James I intended the company to provide a foundation for future settlement. Because of the company's royal support, good ships, and plentiful supplies, New Hampshire's settlements developed into some of the most successful towns of the 1600s.

In 1623, David Thompson, a Scotsman, led another mission to New Hampshire from England. He was joined by two London fish merchants, Edward and Thomas Hilton, and together they established two early fishing settlements. One was named Little Harbor, which would later become Rye. The other, eight miles to the north, was called Northam, which is today's Dover. Soon other settlers arrived, drawn by the rich supply of fish in the waters off the coast of New Hampshire.

The settlers remained at peace with local Native Americans, mostly Abenaki and Pennacooks, who traded animal **pelts** for European items such as clothing and kettles. Many early settlers in the 1600s did not know how to farm, fish, or hunt in New England's rocky land. Native Americans taught the settlers how to fish, hunt animals, grow **maize,** make snowshoes, build canoes, and find **medicinal plants.** The settlers also learned how to cut timber and to farm the poor, rocky soil.

*Benning Wentworth was New Hampshire's colonial governor from 1741 to 1767, the longest tenure of any of the colonies' governors.*

## THE COLONIAL ERA

Governed mostly by the Wentworth family, New Hampshire grew to be a thriving colony. Its economy expanded. The town of Derry made linen fabric, and Portsmouth flourished as a busy port with a growing number of merchants and shipbuilders. Off the coast, fishing boomed. Colonial New Hampshirites made great **profits** by selling salted codfish to Europeans. By 1776, New Hampshire had about 82,000 residents.

# The Portsmouth Alarm

On the night of April 18, 1775, Paul Revere rode from Boston to Lexington and Concord, Massachusetts, to warn of a British raid. The battle of Lexington and Concord marked the beginning of the American Revolution (1775–1783). Nearly five months earlier, on December 13, 1774, Revere rode the Boston Post Road north to Portsmouth, warning its citizens of a gathering of British forces. Because of poor weather, the British did not attack that night. If they had attacked, the "Portsmouth Alarm" might have signaled the start of the Revolution.

## THE AMERICAN REVOLUTION

New Hampshirites played a critical role in the **American Revolution** (1775–1783). Throughout the war, they fought in every important battle, although no battles were fought in New Hampshire itself. Portsmouth became an important port, where three warships for the Revolutionary cause were built. One of these, the *Ranger*, was captained by the famous Revolutionary naval officer John Paul Jones. The *Ranger* sailed to France and then to the coast of Great Britain. Under Jones's leadership, the *Ranger* attacked the coastal town of Whitehaven. The attack did little damage, but the British were upset that the small American navy could attack them at all.

## STATEHOOD

In the summer of 1787, Philadelphia hosted a convention for **delegates** from each colony to consider a new constitution. New Hampshire sent two representatives, Nicholas Gilman and John Langdon. On June 21, 1788, when New Hampshirites ratified, or approved, the convention's constitution, New Hampshire officially became the ninth state to ratify. New Hampshire's favorable vote was especially important. The delegates had agreed that nine of the thirteen states must approve the new constitution before it would become the supreme law of the land.

## THE INDUSTRIAL REVOLUTION

By the time of the **industrial revolution** in the early 1800s, New Hampshire's economy had begun to change. Although its population had grown from 142,000 people in 1790 to 318,000 in 1850, many people were leaving for larger cities or more productive farmland out of state. Those who did not leave headed to New Hampshire's cities to work in the new **textile** mills and shoe factories. The most famous and largest factory was the Amoskeag Manufacturing Company (1835–1935) of Manchester, which would eventually produce millions of miles of cloth, plus locomotives and even fire engines. Because of the Amoskeag Manufacturing Company, the population of Manchester grew from 500 people in 1838 to 10,000 in 1846—about 20 times larger in less than 10 years!

## FAMOUS PEOPLE

**Josiah Bartlett** (1729–1795), colonial leader. Josiah Bartlett was a **Revolutionary War** patriot and the second person to sign the **Declaration of Independence,** after John Hancock. He also served as chief justice of the New Hampshire Supreme Court and was one of the first governors of the state (1790–1794).

*Daniel Webster, one of New Hampshire's most brilliant men, was born in a simple two-room farmhouse.*

**Daniel Webster** (1782–1852), **orator** and statesman. Born in Salisbury (now Franklin), Webster became one of the country's most respected lawyers. He represented New Hampshire in the U.S. House of Representatives from 1813 to 1817. Moving to Massachusetts in 1817, he served as a senator from that state from 1827 to 1841 and again from 1845 to 1850. Later, he was secretary of state under presidents William Henry Harrison, John

Tyler, and Millard Fillmore. As secretary of state, he negotiated the Webster-Ashburton Treaty in 1842, which established the border between Maine and Canada.

**Sarah Josepha Hale** (1788–1879), editor and author. As an editor, Hale entertained Americans with her popular magazine *Godey's Lady's Book,* one of the country's first publications for women. Her poem "Mary Had a Little Lamb" was put to music and became one of the most well known children's songs of all time. She was born in Newport.

**Franklin Pierce** (1804–1869), fourteenth president of the United States (1853–1857). Born in Hillsboro, Pierce is the only president from New Hampshire. He served just before the **Civil War** (1861–1865). During his term in office, the divisions between the northern and southern sections of the country grew worse. Pierce was unable to heal these divisions.

*"Go West, young man," a phrase credited to Greeley, expresses his keen interest in the new western lands.*

**Horace Greeley** (1811–1872), journalist and publisher. Born in Amherst, Greeley became a powerful force in American magazine and newspaper publishing. He founded the *New York Tribune* in 1841, which helped shape Americans' ideas. Greeley used the *New York Tribune* to voice his antislavery views both before and during the Civil War (1861–1865). He ran for president in 1872 but lost and died a few weeks after the election.

**Robert Frost** (1874–1963), poet. Frost won four **Pulitzer Prizes** writing poems about **rural** New England. In 1960, Congress awarded Frost a gold medal "in recognition of his poetry, which has enriched the culture of the United States and the philosophy of the world." He lived in Derry and Franconia.

**Alan B. Shepard, Jr.** (1923–1998), astronaut. On May 5, 1961, Shepard became the first American to travel in space. His spacecraft was named *Freedom 7.* He was also the fifth man to walk on the moon, which he did in 1971 while commanding *Apollo 14,* **NASA's** third **lunar** mission. He was born in East Derry.

**David Souter** (1939– ), Supreme Court justice. Souter joined the New Hampshire State Supreme Court in 1983. In 1990, President George H. W. Bush (1989–1993) nominated him to the U.S. Supreme Court. He grew up in Weare.

**Carlton Fisk** (1947– ), baseball player. Fisk, a Boston Red Sox catcher, was a ten-time all-star player and also holds the major league record for home runs by a catcher—351. His home run in game six of the 1975 World Series gave the Red Sox a seven to six victory over the Cincinnati Reds and provided one of baseball's most memorable moments. Fisk was reared in Charlestown.

*Christa McAuliffe was chosen from among more than 11,000 educators to enter NASA's astronaut training program.*

**Christa McAuliffe** (1948–1986), teacher and astronaut. Selected by NASA, the U.S. space agency, to be the first teacher to travel in space, McAuliffe became the pride of New Hampshire. She had planned to teach two lessons from space. Tragedy struck, however, on January 28, 1986, when she and six other astronauts were killed aboard the space shuttle *Challenger* after it exploded seconds after liftoff. Today, Concord, where she taught, is home to the Christa McAuliffe Planetarium, named in her honor.

# The Old Man of the Mountain

**T**he unique rock formation known as the Old Man of the Mountain served as one of New Hampshire's most famous symbols until 2003.

## A NATURAL FORMATION

Located on Profile Mountain, above Franconia Notch in the White Mountains, stood a rock formation made of five ledges of Conway red granite. Stacked on top of one another, the rocks, about 40 feet high and 25 feet wide, jutted about 1,200 feet from the side of the mountain. In profile, that is, from its side, the rock formation resembled a man's face. In about 1805, New Hampshire's people began calling the formation Old Man of the Mountain.

*Visitors came from across the country to see the Old Man of the Mountain. After May 2003, however, the Old Man was gone. All that remained was a pile of rocks at the base of the mountain.*

# The Great Stone Face

Nathaniel Hawthorne, a famous writer of the mid-1800s, wrote a short story inspired by the Old Man of the Mountain. Titled *The Great Stone Face,* it is a tale of a young boy who dedicates his entire life to the Old Man, which looks down upon the lad every day. The story teaches patience and wisdom.

The process that created the face began more than 200 million years ago. Erosion, the slow wearing away of the Earth's surface by wind, rain, or glaciers, sculpted the rocks into a unique form.

## A CHERISHED SYMBOL

A source of pride for New Hampshirites, the famous face symbolized their tough, independent ways. Because of this association, the famous profile of the Old Man was chosen to represent New Hampshire on its state quarter, minted in 2000.

On May 3, 2003, the 700-ton Old Man crashed to the ground below. Erosion, the same force that created the formation, caused its end. New Hampshire's people were shocked by the loss. Some people have called for the face to be rebuilt. Others have suggested a monument to honor the Old Man. One clever idea is to install **viewfinders** at the mountain's base to recreate the Old Man's image. By looking through the viewfinder, the Old Man would appear on the mountainside as if the rock formation had never fallen. Will New Hampshirites choose viewfinders to honor the Old Man? If they do, this use of viewfinders would be a first in the nation.

New Hampshire's governor remembered the Old Man this way: "It was the ultimate symbol of those who would 'Live Free or Die.' And while that symbol may have fallen, that spirit still remains."

# New Hampshire's State Government

**N**ew Hampshire's government is based in Concord, the capital. The state is governed by a constitution, a plan of government approved by the state's people.

New Hampshire's government is similar to the **federal government** in Washington, D.C. Like the federal government, New Hampshire's government is made up of three branches—the legislative, the executive, and the judicial.

## THE LEGISLATIVE BRANCH

New Hampshire's **legislature,** called the General Court, makes the state's laws. It consists of two houses—the

*Concord, the state capital, was first settled in 1733 and named Rumford.*

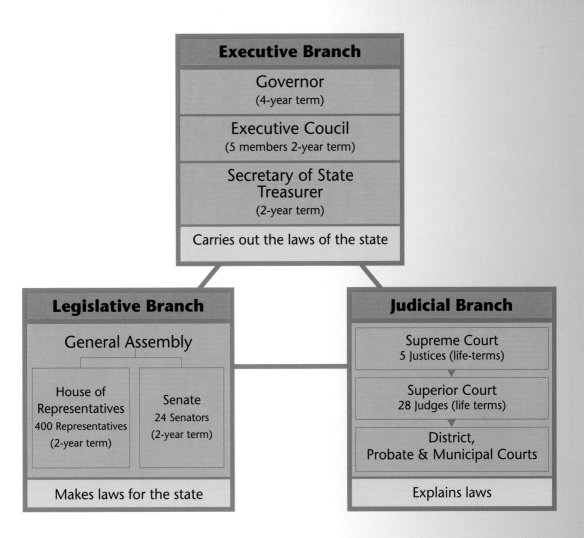

**Executive Branch**

Governor
(4-year term)

Executive Coucil
(5 members 2-year term)

Secretary of State
Treasurer
(2-year term)

Carries out the laws of the state

**Legislative Branch**

General Assembly

House of Representatives
400 Representatives
(2-year term)

Senate
24 Senators
(2-year term)

Makes laws for the state

**Judicial Branch**

Supreme Court
5 Justices (life-terms)

Superior Court
28 Judges (life terms)

District,
Probate & Municipal Courts

Explains laws

senate and the house of representatives. The senate's 24 members are elected to two-year terms. The house's 400 members make it the largest state legislative body in the country. In 1776, New Hampshire's leaders fixed a ratio between the number of representatives and the state's population. As the number of people in the state grew, so, too, did the number of representatives. In 1942, legislators limited the house to no more than 400 members, with no fewer than 375. Representatives are elected to two-year terms. New Hampshire's legislators are not restricted by term limits.

## THE EXECUTIVE BRANCH

New Hampshire's executive branch enforces the state's laws and runs the state from day to day. The governor is the head of this branch. He or she is elected to a four-year term and is not restricted by term limits.

New Hampshire's executive branch is unique because it has, along with a governor, a five-member executive council. Each member is elected to a two-year term and represents his or her region in the state. Council members assist the governor with appointing state officials and awarding state contracts. They also approve spending for most of the state budget.

## THE JUDICIAL BRANCH

The judicial branch decides how the state's laws apply to particular cases. New Hampshire's judicial branch includes the district court, the superior court, and the supreme court.

District courts, located in 36 cities and towns across the state, are New Hampshire's community courts. District court cases involve families, children, small claims, minor crimes, and civil disputes in which the disputed amount does not exceed $25,000.

The superior court has jurisdiction over many types of cases, including criminal and civil cases. It is the only part of the New Hampshire court system that holds jury trials. In an average year, superior court judges hear more than 50,000 cases. Almost half of the cases involve family issues, including divorce, legal separation, child custody, and child support. The superior court is staffed by a chief justice and 27 justices.

The New Hampshire Supreme Court, which is made up of a chief justice and four associate justices, meets in Concord. It is the state's only **appellate court.** The supreme court may choose the cases it hears, except for murder cases, which the law requires it to hear.

*The New Hampshire Supreme Court heads the state's judicial branch.*

# New Hampshire's Culture

## YANKEE INDEPENDENCE AND FREEDOM

With their motto, Live Free or Die, and their choice of the stone face of the Old Man of the Mountain for their state quarter, it is clear the people of New Hampshire have long embraced an image of strength, liberty, and **self-reliance.** The first settlers were hard-working people, able to overcome difficulties of weather and unfertile soil. Today's residents are no different. They still enjoy their rugged image and value their freedom above all. Self-reliance is so important to New Hampshirites that each town holds town meetings so that citizens can come together to discuss community issues. Among the topics discussed at town meetings are the election of public officials, the town budget, and local business.

## FESTIVALS AND FAIRS

New Hampshirites celebrate the diversity of people and cultures in the state with festivals and fairs throughout

*Town meetings are often held in small country stores, which are a big part of small town life in New Hampshire.*

*Visitors enjoy the mountain scenery and the crafts at the Fall Festival in Lincoln.*

the year. They also celebrate the state's history and wildlife.

The Portsmouth Festival, held the last weekend in September, celebrates the city's connection to the sea. The performance of music and work songs once heard aboard sailing ships recalls life in the 1700s and 1800s. Musicians have come from as far away as Great Britain to join the local performers.

The Lincoln Fall Craft Festival brings thousands of people to the White Mountains each October when the fall leaves are changing colors. The festivial features an arts and crafts show, railroad rides, food, and live music.

More than 30,000 people come to the Hillsborough Balloon Festival each summer. Clowns, bands, and floats parade through the town of Hillsborough to kick off the festival.

The town of Errol, in northern New Hampshire near the Maine border, celebrates the varied ecology of the area with the Umbagog Wildlife Festival each year. Named for nearby Umbagog Lake, the festival not only provides food and fun but also educates people and works to preserve the environment. A diversity of wildlife thrives in the unique habitat near the lake. Visitors have an opportunity to study and enjoy the animals. They can also learn how to build a bat house, tour the lake in a **pontoon boat,** or just enjoy the rural scenery.

# New Hampshire's Food

## BOUNTY FROM THE SEA

Among the many creatures that live along the New Hampshire coast, some of the most common and tasty are clams. Whether they are steamed or eaten raw on the half-shell, cooked in chowder, or deep-fried and served as a sandwich, clams have long been a popular food in New Hampshire.

Another delicacy caught off the coast of New Hampshire is lobster. Today, lobster is one of the most expensive shellfish. Lobster was not always such a luxury food. In the 1600s, when Europeans first arrived on North American shores, they thought lobsters were disgusting. Lobsters were sometimes used as garden fertilizer and to feed prisoners. Moreover, during the **American Revolution**

*Steamed clams are dipped in broth (to remove any remaining sand) and butter.*

# Maple Bread Pudding

**Have an adult help you with this recipe.**

1 tablespoon butter
3 cups fresh breadcrumbs
2 cups warm milk
1 cup maple syrup

4 eggs, beaten
2 tablespoons sugar
1 teaspoon vanilla extract
¼ teaspoon salt
½ teaspoon nutmeg
¼ cup raisins

Preheat oven to 350°F. Melt the butter and then pour it into a 1½-quart casserole dish. Next, stir in the breadcrumbs. Pour the warm milk over the breadcrumbs and let soak for 10 to 12 minutes. Pour the maple syrup over the mixture and stir gently. In a separate bowl, combine eggs, sugar, vanilla, salt, and nutmeg. Beat well  and then stir in raisins. Pour this mixture over the bread mixture. Bake in a 350°F oven for 45 to 55 minutes or until a knife inserted in the center comes out clean. (Note: Be sure to place the casserole dish in a pan of hot water in the oven. Water should come halfway up the side of the casserole dish.)

(1775–1783), American forces insulted the red-coated British soldiers by calling them "lobsterbacks." A century later, though, this opinion changed when European royalty and the wealthy began to eat lobster. Hampton, Portsmouth, and Rye are now the main centers in New Hampshire where lobsters are processed.

## MAPLE SYRUP

Maple syrup, a popular food item with a long history in New Hampshire, is a sweet, thick syrup taken from the sap of certain types of maple trees. Forty gallons of sap are needed to make one gallon of maple syrup. New Hampshire produces an average of 75,000 gallons of it each year.

# New Hampshire's Folklore and Legends

**E**ach state has its own unique myths, folktales, and legends. Legends are stories handed down from generation to generation that may have some historical basis although it cannot be proven.

## OLD MAN MOSES

One New Hampshire legend tells the story of Old Man Moses, who found twelve turkeys sitting on his fence and wished to have them for dinner. Throwing his ax at them, he hit a branch above the fence instead. The branch fell and knocked all the birds into the pond below. Old Man Moses jumped into the pond after them, and as his coat opened under

*Old Man Moses, a man with a large appetite and a little bit of luck on his side, was able to find a week's worth of food in almost no time at all.*

the water, he caught a great many fish. Having retrieved all twelve turkeys and caught a number of fish, he was proud of the fact that he had found a week's worth of dinner in less than ten minutes. The point of this legend is that New Hampshire provides all a person needs to live happily. It also suggests that its residents are ingenious and independent and make the most out of any opportunity without needing help from others.

## THE DEVIL AND DANIEL WEBSTER

A famous New Hampshire story centers on one of the state's most respected natives, Daniel Webster. This story by Stephen Vincent Benét (1898–1943), a U.S. poet and writer, is about a struggling New Hampshire farmer, Jabez Stone. Stone works hard, but his crops fail, and he has bad luck. One day, he swears that he would sell his soul to the devil if he could only become successful. Soon the devil arrives dressed as a stranger, and Stone agrees to sign over his soul. Years pass, and Stone becomes rich and influential in politics, but the devil eventually returns to claim Stone's soul. Afraid, Stone turns to the most famous lawyer of the day, a fellow New Hampshirite, Daniel Webster. Webster agrees to take the case and, in a dramatic trial scene, convinces the judge and jury to let Stone break his contract and go free. The devil is defeated. Webster, true to his image, saved the day.

Benét's story illustrates the power and respect Webster enjoyed in the United States in his lifetime. As Webster was from New Hampshire, the story further shows the tough and intelligent ways of the state's people.

# New Hampshire's Sports Teams

## ATHLETIC TEAMS

New Hampshire's only professional team is a minor league team, the Nashua Pride, a member of the Atlantic League of Professional Baseball Clubs. The league was founded in 1998. Pride plays at Holman Stadium in Nashua. Built in 1937, Holman Stadium is famous for hosting the first racially mixed team in modern times, the Nashua Dodgers.

Many New Hampshirites follow university sports teams. One team of particular note is the University of New Hampshire men's hockey team. In 2003, the UNH Wildcats won the Hockey East Championship Tournament in Boston, Massachusetts, for the second time in a row. In that tournament, they defeated the Boston University Terriers one to zero, posting the first shutout in championship history.

*Former Wildcat Jason Krog (class of 1999) won the 1999 Hobey Baker Memorial Award, given annually to the best college hockey player in the country.*

## WINTER SPORTS

In winter, residents of New Hampshire enjoy ice fishing on any one of New Hampshire's many frozen lakes and rivers. To ice fish, a person first finds a frozen lake, drills a hole in the ice six to twelve inches deep, and then drops a baited hook and waits for a fish to bite.

Another popular winter sport in New Hampshire is skiing, the state sport. There are three main types of skiing. One is alpine skiing, also known as downhill skiing. A second is Nordic skiing, which consists of cross-country skiing and ski jumping. The third is freestyle, or stunt, skiing. Bode Miller, of Franconia, is one of the best alpine skiers in the world. He finished second in the world in the World Cup standings in 2002–2003. At the 2002 Winter Olympics, Miller collected two silver medals.

*In the last decade, snowboarding has become a favorite pastime for winter-sport enthusiasts in New Hampshire.*

# New Hampshire's Businesses and Products

## FARM PRODUCTS

Agriculture has been a part of New Hampshire's history since settlers first arrived almost 400 years ago. Today, farmers in the state grow many different crops, from Christmas trees to crispy apples, blueberries, and sweet corn. Farmers also breed livestock, especially cows and sheep, and produce specialty goods such as maple syrup and jellies and jams. Farming in New Hampshire provides more than just state income. (It earns $675 million for the state each year.) Each farm's fields, pastures, silos, and barns provide a contrast to urban development. The fact that so many landowners have decided to continue farming has kept urban sprawl from taking over the countryside. With 2,700 farms covering more than 460,000 acres, much of the state has retained the quiet feel of the country.

*New Hampshire has approximately 19,000 milk-producing cows.*

New Hampshire differs from most of the rest of the United States because its agricultural industry is growing. While the state supports fewer dairy farms than it once did, a new industry, ornamental **horticulture,** which specializes in greenhouse flowers and plants, brings in hundreds of million of dollars annually. The horticulture industry employs 5,100 workers.

New Hampshire's apple crop earns about $8 million a year for the state. Apple orchards produce almost one million bushels of apples that are sold throughout the United States and Europe. Apple cider, a relatively new industry in New Hampshire, has also become a valuable product for many of the state's apple farmers.

Today, about 190 dairy farms produce more than 40 million gallons of milk each year in New Hampshire. Dairies occupy 400,000 acres of New Hampshire land. Like apples, dairy products are one of the state's most profitable agricultural products.

*Franconia Notch State Park is a spectacular moutain pass that extends to Echo Lake at the north.*

## TOURISM

New Hampshire has thousands of miles of rivers within its borders. With more than 40,000 miles of rivers and 1,300 lakes, it is one of the wettest states in the nation. With its majestic mountains and its meadows and forests, New Hampshire is a favorite vacation spot for many people.

Wolfeboro is home to the oldest summer resort in America, yet tourism in New Hampshire began to grow only in the 1880s, when railroads brought sightseers from Boston and Portland. New Hampshire's natural beauty attracted artists, poets, writers, and scientists, as well as curious visitors. Business leaders built hotels along the coast and in the White Mountains. People came from across the United States and Europe to enjoy the luxuries of the resorts, such as the Mount Washington Hotel. Others camped outdoors or stayed in rustic cabins. By the early 1900s, tourism was a profitable and growing industry in the state.

Throughout the 1920s and 1930s, tourists came by car to sightsee and to look for antiques and handcrafted goods, such as quilts or jellies. By the 1930s, visitors were also coming to New Hampshire each winter to enjoy a new activity—skiing.

Today, millions of people arrive each year to ski, hike, walk New Hampshire's old town streets, splash in lakes, or just relax on its beaches. Tourism has become an important part of New Hampshire's economy. New Hampshire ranks seventh nationally in terms of the **revenue** it earns from tourism, each year drawing in more than $8.6 billion. Tourism also provides 65,000 residents with jobs.

*Tourists visiting the New Hampshire Farm Museum can view its extensive collection of historic farm tools and implements in buildings dating from 1780 to 1900.*

# Attractions and Landmarks

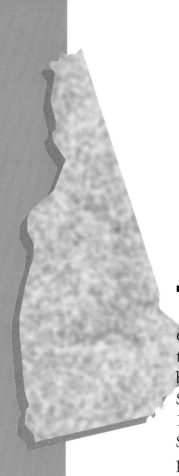

**T**ourism is a successful industry in New Hampshire because of the state's rich history and natural splendor. The town of Bretton Woods, near Mount Washington, combines both aspects. A millionaire railroad owner, Joseph Stickney, opened the Mount Washington Hotel there in 1902. Once the largest wooden building in New England, Stickney spared no expense in its construction. He imported 250 Italian craftsmen to work on the grounds. Even today, it has its own telephone system and post office. When the doors finally opened on July 28, 1902, the Mount Washington Hotel had a staff of 350.

## The Bretton Woods Conference

In 1944, the Mount Washington Hotel hosted the Bretton Woods Conference, a meeting at which world leaders decided international policies about post–**World War II** economics. Both the **World Bank** and the **International Monetary Fund** were created at the Bretton Woods Conference.

Because the Mount Washington Hotel was so luxurious, it soon became a desirable place to visit. Among its guests were English Prime Minister Winston Churchill, inventor Thomas Edison, and baseball great Babe Ruth. In 1975, the hotel was registered on the National Register of Historic Places and the surrounding 6,400 acres became part of the White Mountain National Forest.

New Hampshire is a state known for its authors. People can visit their homes to see how they lived and where they wrote. Two New Hampshire authors are the poets e.e. cummings (1894–1962) and Robert Frost (1874–1963). For much of his life, e.e. cummings (whose name is usually spelled with lowercase letters) lived in Silver Lake. The farm where Robert Frost grew up and wrote many of his poems, including "Stopping by Woods on a Snowy Evening," is located in Derry. He later moved to Franconia, where he published three books and won a **Pulitzer Prize.**

The Strawbery Banke Museum in Portsmouth is an important landmark. In 1630, the British settled a ten-acre

*Tourists enjoy a sunny afternoon at Strawbery Banke.*

# Places to see in New Hampshire

area, which was named for the wild strawberries growing along the banks of the Piscataqua River. The area was renamed Portsmouth in 1653, and in the following centuries, it became a thriving port and shipbuilding center. Today, the original location is an outdoor history museum, as well as an important archaeological site in which many old colonial artifacts, such as pottery and household furnishings, have been discovered.

The home of John Paul Jones, the famous **Revolutionary War** naval officer, is also a popular tourist stop. In 1782, while waiting for the completion of his ship *Amer-*

*ica,* John Paul Jones stayed at the Portsmouth inn of Sarah Purcell. The house is now the property of the Portsmouth Historical Society. Visitors to the inn can see what life was like at the time of the **American Revolution** (1775–1783).

Located in the Canterbury Hills of New Hampshire, in the southeastern region of the state, is the Canterbury Shaker Village. The Shakers, a religious group that originated in England, arrived in the colonies in 1774 seeking religious freedom. They believed in common ownership of property and a simple way of life. They did not believe in marriage or having children of their own. However, they often cared for orphans within their communities. Other people called them Shakers because they quivered and shook at certain points in their religious services. In Canterbury, as elsewhere in the Northeast, they established a successful community, which once covered 4,000 acres and included 100 buildings. Today, 24 buildings remain on 700 acres. The last Shaker to live there died in 1992.

## Shaker Furniture

The Shakers believed in simplicity and self-reliance. They were also very ingenious—they invented the circular saw, a type of washing machine, flat brooms, and the first metal pen. They are particularly famous for their simple but strong wooden furniture, all of which was crafted by hand.

*The Conway Scenic Railroad was built in 1874.*

The Conway Scenic Railroad, the historic train that takes passengers on tours of the Mount Washington valley, was built by the Portsmouth Great Falls & Conway Railroad. It originally transported passengers and mail between Conway and North Conway. Today, from Conway, it offers an 11-mile round-trip tour of farms and rivers, a 21-mile round-trip tour of mountainside scenery, and a tour of Crawford Notch, with its bluffs and steep ravines. Visitors can see most of the depot's original layout, including the ticket office, waiting rooms, and telegraph equipment, all of which remain in fine condition.

The Kancamagus Highway is named after a Pennacook chief (his name means "fearless one") who lived in colonial New Hampshire in the 1680s. The highway runs through the White Mountains National Forest and climbs nearly 3,000 feet alongside Mount Kancamagus. Many people consider it to be the most scenic road in the state, with its magnificent pine trees along each side, its view of the Swift River below, and in fall, its colorful display of foliage. It stretches 38½ miles, from Lincoln to Conway. Each year tourists drive the highway, also known as Route 112, to take in the natural beauty that New Hampshire offers.

# Map of New Hampshire

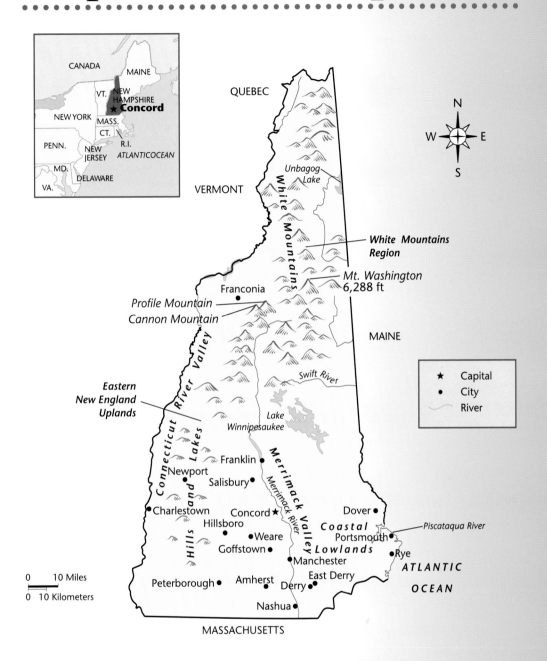

CANADA
MAINE
VT.
NEW
HAMPSHIRE
NEW YORK
★ Concord
MASS.
CT.
PENN.
R.I.
NEW
JERSEY
ATLANTICOCEAN
MD.
DELAWARE
VA.

QUEBEC

N
W        E
S

VERMONT

Unbagog
Lake

White Mountains

White Mountains
Region

Mt. Washington
6,288 ft

Franconia

Profile Mountain
Cannon Mountain

MAINE

Swift River

Eastern
New England
Uplands

Lake
Winnipesaukee

★ Capital
• City
∿ River

Franklin
Newport
Salisbury

Charlestown
Concord ★
Hillsboro
Weare
Goffstown
Peterborough
Amherst
Manchester
Derry
East Derry
Nashua

Dover

Coastal
Portsmouth
Lowlands
Rye

Piscataqua River

ATLANTIC
OCEAN

Connecticut River Valley

Hills and Lakes

Merrimack Valley

Merrimack River

0   10 Miles
0   10 Kilometers

MASSACHUSETTS

# Glossary

**American Revolution** the war in which the thirteen American colonies won independence from Great Britain (1775–1783)

**amphibian** a cold-blooded animal, such as a newt, frog, or toad that lives on the land and breeds in the water

**appellate court** a court that holds the power to review the decisions of other courts

**archaeologists** social scientists who study the cultural remains of earlier peoples

**artifacts** items such as pottery, arrowheads, and tools produced by earlier cultures

**Civil War** the war fought between the northern states, usually called the Union, and the southern states, the Confederacy, over issues such as states' rights and slavery (1861–1865)

**Declaration of Independence** the document in which the thirteen American colonies formally announced their freedom from Great Britain

**delegate** a person who represents others

**ethnic** relating to large groups of people who share common traits or customs

**federal government** the national government

**feldspar** a type of rock that contains aluminum

**hardy** strong, able to withstand poor conditions

**horticulture** the commercial growing of ornamental plants and shrubs

**industrial revolution** the rapid shift in society that began in the late 1800s, when manufacturing moved from the home to the factory

**International Monetary Fund** an international organization, established by the United Nations, to promote economic cooperation between countries

**legislature** a group of elected people who make laws for a state or a country

**lunar** relating to the moon

**maize** a type of corn grown by Native Americans

**medicinal plants** herbs or flowers believed to help cure illnesses

**monarchy** a country ruled by a king or a queen

**NASA** National Aeronautic and Space Administration, an agency of the United States government that is responsible for the nation's space program

**orator** a person skilled in public speaking

**pelts** the skin and fur taken from dead animals

**pontoon boat** a type of boat with a flat bottom

**profit** the money that is earned on an investment

**Pulitzer Prize** a well-known prize awarded for outstanding writing or journalism

**quarry** a place from where stone or rock is removed

**quartz** a type of mineral, often found in granite quarries

**revenue** government income

**Revolutionary War** another name for the American Revolution (1775–1783), the war in which the thirteen American colonies won independence from Great Britain

**rural** relating to the country

**self-government** a state or area that makes its own laws

**self-reliance** depending on oneself for survival

**textile** cloth or fabric

**viewfinders** devices that, when looked through, show an image or picture against a natural background

**World War II** the war (1939–1945) between the Allies (Great Britain, France, Russia, the United States) and the Axis (Germany, Italy, Japan)

**World Bank** an agency of the United Nations established in 1945 to make loans to member nations

# More Books to Read

Harvey, Bonnie Carman. *Daniel Webster: "Liberty and Union, Now and Forever."* Berkeley Heights, N.J.: Enslow Publishers, Inc., 2001.

Mattern, Joanne. *New Hampshire: The Granite State.* Milwaukee, WI: World Almanac Library, 2003.

Moore, Kay. *If You Lived at the Time of the American Revolution.* New York, N.Y.: Scholastic Trade, 1998.

Otfinoski, Steven. *New Hampshire (Celebrate the States).* Tarrytown, N.Y.: Benchmark Books, 1999.

Stein, R. Conrad. *New Hampshire (America the Beautiful: Second Series).* Danbury, CT: Children's Press, 2000.

# Index

# About the Authors

Peter Melman earned his Ph.D. in English from the University of Louisiana-Lafayette. His fiction, nonfiction, and poetry have been published nationally in more than a dozen literary journals. He learned about New Hampshire from his travels and from attending summer camp on beautiful Lake Winnipesaukee for five consecutive summers during his youth.

D. J. Ross is a writer with more than 25 years of experience in education. He has lived in New England and still frequently visits New Hampshire. He now lives in the Midwest with his three basset hounds.